winter dogs
DREW BLANCHARD

salmonpoetry

Published in 2011 by
Salmon Poetry
Cliffs of Moher, County Clare, Ireland
Website: www.salmonpoetry.com
Email: info@salmonpoetry.com

Copyright © Drew Martin Blanchard, 2011

ISBN 978-1-907056-62-8

All rights reserved. No part of this publication may be reproduced or transmitted in any form or by any means, electronic or mechanical, including photography, recording, or any information storage or retrieval system, without permission in writing from the publisher. The book is sold subject to the condition that it shall not, by way of trade or otherwise, be lent, resold or otherwise circulated without the publisher's prior consent in any form of binding or cover other than that in which it is published and without a similar condition, including this condition, being imposed on the subsequent purchaser.

Cover artwork: *"What Remains" by Nichole Maury is borrowed from an installation of 36 prints*
Cover design: *Deep Sea Studios*
Typesetting: *Siobhán Hutson*

for keeping each other
alive through rain,
cold, pain, and night

Acknowledgements

Grateful acknowledgement to the editors of the following magazines and anthologies for their support:

Notre Dame Review: "Wrecking the Orpheum" & "The Allerton Hotel, Chicago"
Best New Poets 2006: "Idle"
Blue Canary: "Desert of Weightless Clouds"
Flat City Anthology: "Union Street"
Best New Poets 2008: "Watching Fire"
Meridian: "From Nowhere Near Mt. Hood, Oregon"
Blue Canary: "Winter Dogs"
Guernica/a magazine of art & politics: "Flocks of Never"
Copper Nickel: "Silent"
Gulf Stream: "Two Mornings on Avenida 9 de Julio"
Lake Effect: A Journal of the Literary Arts: "Moving"
Blackbird /an online journal of literature and the arts: "From Grace to Goshen," "Sweethearts," "Son," "For the Record," & "Not Whiskey"
Booth: "We Do This," "January Now," & "Mine Own Baudelaire"

I would like to thank Jessie Lendennie and Siobhán Hutson for their generous support and hard work. Thanks also to Erica Wright and Kathleen Rooney for their time and kind words. I would also like to thank the MFA program at OSU, especially the guidance of Kathy, Andrew, Erin, Michelle, Lee M., and Lee K., and in memory of David Citino. I am grateful too for the support of the PhD program and Graduate School at UWM, with special thanks to José, Brenda, Rebecca, Kim, Liam, and the late James Liddy. I would like to extend personal gratitude to Jim Chapson for his assistance and for his careful eye. And a throwback thanks to Karen for the "Wasteland" and more, and to Jim and Shuata. And finally I would like to thank the following friends and writers for their smart and thoughtful attention to the book as it took shape: Jolie, Maria, Derrick, Joe, Kelly, Jason, Dan, and Sean.

Contents

Not Whiskey	13
Watching Fire	14
Wrecking the Orpheum	15
From Nowhere Near Mt. Hood	16
Not Crows	17
Silent	18
Son	20
Muscle	21
For the Record	22
Not Animal	23
Union Street	25
The Early Dark	26
Firmament	29
January Outtake	31
Sweethearts	32
Binding	33
Moving	34
Not Magic	36
New Orleans	38
We Do This	39
Mine Own Baudelaire	41
Cafés are Dying	43
For Your Horse	45
Liddy's Prayer Card	46

It	49
Idle	50
Winter Dogs	51
Night	53
New York	54
Before the Bookcase	55
Not Anointed	56
The Allerton Hotel, Chicago	57
January	58
Hunting Eagles	59
Two Mornings on Avenida 9 de Julio	60
Will He Not Recall	62
From Grace to Goshen	63
Flocks of Never	64
Notes	67
About the Author	69

*On the dog's path, my soul came upon
my heart. Shattered, but alive,
dirty, poorly dressed, and filled with love.
On the dog's path, there where no one wants to go.*

  —Roberto Bolaño, *Dirty, Poorly Dressed*

*Because one must give up
What one cannot hold back,
Which becomes something else
With or against the heart—
Wholly forget it,*

*Then beat the bushes
To search without finding
That which must heal us
Of the unknown anguish
We carry with us everywhere.*

  —René Char, *Mourning at Nevons*

winter dogs

Not Whiskey

At dusk—west of Patch Grove—
two bison become an electric fence,
a fox, a question about crossing the street,
yellow circles of fallen leaves, a flower
arrangement that turns love again to lust.
      Four hundred miles east the bison,
lost in wandering, witness a son
bankrupt a bar, bust the town of Black Wolf,
fold the farm as metal folds in train wrecks.
The bison, alone again in wandering,
are not box knives, not crows,
not a soiled sheet, a trailer-park-storm.
They do not go into the woods alone.
They are not a last dance, drunk,
not a blue jay, not whiskey, not a time-clock.

Watching Fire

The blaze of maple's orange and sumac's red
has fallen away, and gingko's golden fans
are all that remain. The earth is ashy now
with leaves, a carpet of crackling death, and yet
I love the feel of life before we retreat
for winter, to breathe the same air again and again.
Last week my neighbor's wife walked out on him.
I know this because he and a fifth
of Johnny Walker didn't go home until
my kitchen windows turned from black to gray
and pink—an autumn sun our final call.
The next day, raking leaves, I heard a crash
from Jerry's house, and then his sweaty head
poked out the back door. Looking wildly around
he dragged, banging and clanking, a bed frame
into the middle of his lawn. Smiling, he walked
back inside. A minute later he returned,
the mattress cut in two; he tossed the pieces
on the broken frame. After a few hours,
a sculpture of shoes and books,
of clothes and kitchen utensils, amassed
in Jerry's backyard.
                        When my parents divorced
I didn't see such passion screaming from them.
I was ten, the same year Father said "it's time,"
my brother and I finally old enough
to help him chop and gather wood. We scoured
ravines behind our house and down to Trout
Creek in search of fallen oaks and elms.
Father cut hundred year old trees into wedges
small enough to chop. Small pieces of dust
and chips clung to his beard and clothes,
cloaking him in what he was dismantling.
The strangest thing I recall the year Mother left,
was that Father, who never wasted the good oak,
our fuel for the stove, built a bonfire that burned
late into the dark of an autumn night.

Wrecking the Orpheum

Above the empty orchestra pit and the gold
ornamental arches, above the hand-carved
theater faces and the blue mosaic columns,
above the glimmering glass of chandeliers,
a century of dust rises to the ceiling before it falls.
      With a crowbar, I pry splintering floorboards
from the stage. I salvage, to the dismay of my boss,
this lacquered wood for the long tenured
Theater Director—his final holding on.
As I lever the hundred-year-old nails, they bend and whine.
In high school I played Mercutio on this stage,
and backstage made love with Juliet. She did not
fumble with the passion as I did.
      Years later, backstage of another theater,
in another city, I experienced my first slow
melt from the needle—the initial taste
as explosive as making love. Now, clean
for six months, home again with steady work,
I am back on stage. As I sweat in the dust I can
almost hear the tiny ring of the curtain bell,
my backstage nervous breath, the whisper
of the audience and the rustle of programs.
      Tonight they'll auction off the theater seats,
doorknobs, pictures of Dvořák, bristly beard
and serious eyes, as he directs the symphony
in 1893. Tomorrow, the wrecking ball, the masonry
and stone will fall, all but the façade, a memoriam,
a gateway to the glass and steel of the new civic center.

From Nowhere Near Mt. Hood

A man wakes up on the floor, cold coffee spilled
beside him in the shape of Florida, he thinks,
or maybe Lake Michigan. On the flimsy line
stretched across his balcony, his underwear and pants
flap against the dirty glass. A trace of perfume
wafts in from the hallway outside, and he thinks
of his ex-wife in New York, pictures her riding
the subway to work, her head and book bouncing
with the rhythm of the train. He pictures the empty
seat beside her, then himself in the empty seat
staring at her closed mouth, the deep creases
in her forehead. In the hall a door slams.
He looks down at the upturned mug,
the coffee, no longer Lake Michigan, but a river
making its way toward his slippers. He had fallen
asleep listening to the woman in the next apartment
practice her violin. He often sat, his shoulders
slumped against the wall, his legs spread
over the floor, listening to her play
the same D major sonata again and again,
never quite getting it right. It begins to rain.
He walks to his desk; the trees outside his window,
glazed and bending, have never looked so strained.
On a postcard to his ex-wife he writes:

Thought you might like this picture of Mt. Hood.
Always wanted to go there, maybe someday.
Moscow is cold, even in the spring.
May or may not go to the symphony tonight. Love You.

Not Crows

She sinks into the bed. He removes
brittle bandages from her legs,
kneels down beside her and rubs
saffron on the seeping wounds. They are
awash now in the honey-hay scent.

Staring at her thighs, he thinks of her
drunk at his brother's wedding and presses harder.
She poisons everything.
              She poisons everything she touches.

She shifts her legs, uses *that language* again.
He turns off the light. She closes her eyes,
sees birds, sparrows she thinks,
not crows, sees her mother hanging
white sheets on the line, sees her
red apron, her calloused hands.

Silent

> *An ordinary miracle:*
> *in the dead of night*
> *the barking of invisible dogs.*
>   —Wisława Szymborska

When your older sister burned
the meatloaf while she bathed
you and was punished
by your father's meaty palm
against her head, the repeated
smack and thud a lesson
in the dislike of all things
burnt, you crouched behind
the bathroom door, still wet,
and cried into your towel.
That night when you cuddled
beside her in bed, your knees tucked in
the small of her back,
the drip of blood from her ears
dried below your pillow
as she gazed out the window
into speckled winter sky.

Or maybe you were the teacher,
who didn't notice the blood
crusted inside your student's ears,
you didn't notice her solemn absence
as your voice raised in anger
when she wouldn't look at you
or write her answer on the board.
And when you finally slammed
your hands down on her desk,
her books and pencils plummeting
to the floor, you saw that she was
not there, not with you
even in your embarrassment.

But maybe you were the one
who burned the meatloaf;
maybe you were the one
who still cooked
for a father who loved you
with a violent swagger.
Maybe you were the one
who still sang, in a soundless
world, to your baby sister
as you bathed her before bed.
And maybe as you lay each night,
your sister asleep beside you,
so close to the window
your breath steamed against the glass,
so close to the night-sky
and shifting trees that you could feel
their sway; and after many nights
without sleep, you could only fall
into dreams with the barking of invisible dogs.

Son

> *I had been thinking of Gabriel,*
> *of the moon-cycle, of the moon shell*
>
> —H.D.

I am moonlight
pale under the bus stop
streetlight. A man in wingtips,
no pants, cups his hand
against my back
to light his Camel.
He walks away,
his shirttails veil
what we must
not see. There are so many things
that will never happen
to me. This is not
one of them. A camel,
though, will never carry me
through any desert.
I will not be a horse
out to pasture; I will
never swim in water
with barracuda or piraña.
I will never swim with gold.
I will never fly blind,
bat-like, at dusk.
I am not moonlight.
I will never give
birth to a son.

Muscle

He forgets her violet
scent, her thick skin,
violent tongue, her lashes like Venus
Flytraps. He forgets the Marchand
floodplains, his flatlands
cut by silt-water flowing south.
He forgets the tin-can
river that cut their feet.
He remembers the tall grass,
empty boxcars, her breath, their last
rustle in summer sheets, the new
moon and becomes
a tadpole in summer
backwater as it sun-dries to dust.

For the Record

I don't remember the color
my wife's hair turns in summer.
She is no longer my wife.
Winter wheat. The sound of a record
when the music ends,
when the needle glides and skips
is the soundtrack to everything
in your brother's backyard.
Swans wandering outside
my grandfather's hospital
window, willows
bending toward water,
away from sky, signified,
for him, nothing but swans
shitting on grass and weepy trees.
Their wings unclipped, the swans'
migration never changed:
spring then autumn then
spring then autumn. I always dance
at dances. I always never stop.

Not Animal

Skittering fingers on rusty
guitar strings, sparks
from steel on steel,
train cars hitching, a fire's
whisper and crack, snow,
the flutter of two
hundred starlings
massing like rain clouds,
is this what keeps us alive?
More than once the earth has fallen
silent, soundless from a tremor
too much for this world.
In these moments, stillness
did not follow. Everywhere
trees whipped and bowed in the wind,
but their leaves said nothing.

If all sounds disappear
we should not make
for cover, nor should we flee
our homes, instead we should
lie down and hope for sound.
First we should hope
for sounds we can't make
out in the middle of the night:
the tick-tick outside our window
that is not animal, not wind
stretching power lines,
sounds seemingly dangerous
yet not dangerous, sounds that can
not be distinguished.
Indistinguishable sounds.
Then we should hope specific:
the snap of eggs frying,

the squeak of not yet
wet enough skin
moving on skin,
the laugh of our mothers:
nasal, guttural, a high squeal
like that of a pig—a sound
we hate, but a sound that makes
us love our mothers even more.
In this moment, do not think
of rain on a tin roof
unless you have heard
the tink and ping
of rain on a tin roof.
Do not imagine the spitting
tea kettle's whistle, a room's
empty echo or the cries
of fatherless children.

Union Street

This morning the bells of Saint Mary's
didn't ring. And the asphalt still holds
puddles and plaster from the burning.
In August, morning is the only cool time
on Union Street, the only time you can walk
barefoot without blistering.

Last night as the steeples churned out
black tower clouds and snowed
paper-thin ashes, we all gazed as our
memories and confessions floated
to the ground. Even Curtis, who spends
everyday painting the street

centerlines with a dry brush he keeps
in a shoebox, stopped to watch parishioners
enamored of the flames: Mr. Kopetsky
the one armed custodian and Mrs. Reshetova,
offering her lemonade and blackberry pie.
The Archbishop performed a vigil

just as the wind sent the blaze
onto the motherhouse. Last night
I dreamed the city was overtaken by crimson
vines—overpowered by sprawling
clematis and ivy, engulfed with daffodils,
clusters of yarrow, delphinium and violet sage.

This morning, as I walk to Paul's Supermarket,
the men in front of Arthur's Resale are throwing
cards as usual, and dipping their neck
towels in ice buckets full of Blatz.
And I can still smell the charcoal in the air
as displaced swallows search for new homes.

The Early Dark

Tonight, scattered books,
green tea now cold,
outside flakes of snow
freeze against my window.
A young mother and daughter,
mid-storm, offer to *shovel
me out*. They are frozen
scarecrows come alive:
their faces wrapped
in purple scarves,
snot quivering in time
with their breathing,
jeans frosted grayish-white
past the knee. On the hard-
cushioned sofa that was once
your favorite spot, I listen
as they chop and grind
against concrete and ice.

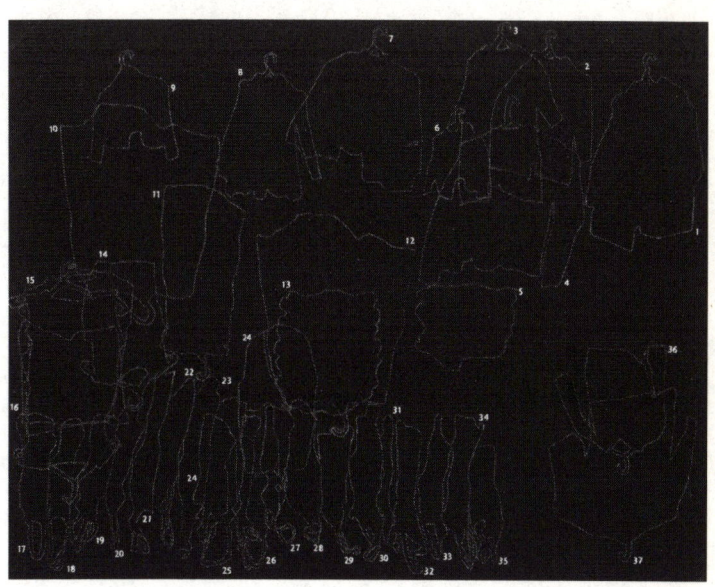

Firmament

    We all dance naked
in television's blue light.
    What else can we do?

    Broken window glass
hidden in snow. Winter wind
    blows in. Someone's gone.

    Dreaming of the beach:
sand in our hair, teeth, crotch, beer.
    Cloudless nights: homeless freeze.

    Seed and ash buried
under snow. Under blue skies
    the lake steams all day.

    Black sky peppered white.
What are we against the cold?
    A mouse in a field.

    We never leave home:
grandmother's watches and rings
    drawers of coins, frayed socks.

    Planetarium's
pinhole lights, our projections,
    our constellation?

    Empty gray feeder,
blue jays, finches, cardinals, crows,
    flock in naked oaks.

A broom, a dishcloth:
how many years does it take?
　　Pantries full of soup.

　　The back door slams shut.
Words thrown like barroom bottles
　　break in evening air.

January Outtake

In April it didn't rain and you
    called it blood-month.
        You mouthed the words
bone-balloon and I drew
        stick figures of zoo animals.
    You wrote questions on steamy
        bathroom mirrors
          about relativity, about time and then
            answered your questions
        in octagons and absence.
    In July you pointed to my stick
figure animals, said that I forgot
        faux-rock caves for bears, monkey bars,
          designated smoking areas.
    I thought of empty corners and unused
spaces in abandoned barns. I said something
    about leaving
doors unlocked and the awful
    shape of silos.
        January now and you
talk of sandstorms, make
      lists of animals and plants
you've never touched. I raise
    an eyebrow and play,
for three days straight,
    happy birthday
        on my new piano.

Sweethearts

There is no wind in the barely lit
afternoon bar. The man next to me
says to the woman on the stool next to him,
"I think you and your fish
should move in with me."
The woman smiles, says nothing,
but offers him her hands; their eyes
grow wide like fields of Iowa corn,
like green fields of soy before they turn
autumn rust. And as their hearts
sit naked on the bar, thumping,
bloody for all to see, I think how hard
it must be to move a fish.

Binding

Because he wanted more
than to feed his family
on the flesh of horses,
they moved from Warsaw:
hunger, trains, Atlantic sway,
distant harbor lights,
New York, stale bread,
yesterday's broth. Food's ache
like putting on shoes,
like breathing. He never softened
stories for children's ears. *To sacrifice a son
is not courageous, it's obedient.*
Abraham's almost-sacrifice,
his favorite. He was asked by God
to stay in Stalinist starvation,
but he didn't bind the ram,
instead, family in tow,
he came to America.
Each day he'd walk downtown
to repent at St. Raphael's.
Inside the empty cathedral
he knelt in front of Christ
crucified, the unforgiving
branch of rose, spikes through flesh,
thinking how St. Casimir
would kneel for hours
before the locked
doors of churches
each night to pray,
but shifting on sore
knees, he could not
confess to anything.

Moving

We carried, through the night, suitcases and boxes,
my father straining, forehead slick with sweat.
His wife, the third one since my mother left,
had dumped his records, golf clubs, and fishing poles
into the pond. "Everything he loved
more than me," she said. Even his '62
Austin Healy—the roof glinting like a wet wreck
in the moonlight. "I have a new island
to fish from," he joked. But then we worked
in silence, cramming his clothes and paper work
into the Cadillac, before collapsing on the lawn.
As we sat under the branches of a swaying oak,
he began to disappear. His languid frame
hollowed out like bones of birds. When he was thin
he looked like my mother; strange how the booze
brought them together in a bizarre mirror
of each other. But this is not what he remembers
of middle age, of my youth. He's better served
now by memories of our fishing
along the Mississippi; and his favorite story
of how I learned, when I was ten,
the meaning of four letter words
from the walls inside a limestone cave.
The vaulted rocks were covered with names
of lovers, drawings of pussies and penises,
and strange protests of love. *Shelly and Danny forever*,
and *FUCK YOU DAN* written overtop.
My father, smiling, let me read the words aloud
only once, and then I promised never
to repeat them. Their power existed, he said,
in carefully chosen moments. The first careful
moment I heard these words: my second stepmother
unleashing them, screaming, while packing her bags.
In the hallway outside their bedroom, my father stood,

rejecting, I imagine, every fiery syllable.
Now he doesn't use many words; he has fallen
into silence the way a forgotten barn twists
on its foundation until it collapses
under the weight of itself.

Not Magic

Newly adopted babies from Russia,
    Katya and Valentina,
        now Katy and Valerie,

cry out like the shrill of a troubled
    blue jay. Outside my window,
        a silhouette of mountains

under a pink dusting of clouds.
    Along the wing, mud-stained boot prints
        crisscross like a skater's

figure eight. Close to the plane's
    body, the tracks spread out,
        disappear over the edge.

I imagine falling from the wing
    into a storm of snow and hail,
        imagine being engulfed in cold,

blinded by wind and crystalline ice, and how
    wrapped in such weather,
        it might not feel like falling at all;

like a magician's assistant that is vanished
    yet not gone for good,
        how she does not feel

severed by the saw that cuts her in two.
    In Moscow, a warm summer rain fell
        as I boarded the plane. And you,

rain-water wet, drenched
    like the time you jumped,
        fully dressed, into the January lake,

waved like the mayor at a ticker-tape parade.
    You, though, are not the mayor.
        You are not the magician either.

Under the wave of your wand
    I did not vanish, but unlike the assistant
        who remains unscathed

by the saw's blade, I am vanquished,
    no longer whole. The twins and their parents
        are now asleep. Outside my window

the whisper of clouds have dissipated and the sun
    glares on the green side of the mountains.
        My Aunt Sophie, whose husband died

on their honeymoon, said that she and Frank
    formed a mountain. He was the ocean side,
        lush and fertile. She was the desert of weightless clouds.

New Orleans

after the photograph "Blind DeDe Pierce – one of the last old New Orleans Jazz men," by Leonard Freed

I imagine breasts
behind cotton
camisoles brushing
your sinewy back,
leaving lemon balm
trails that burned
your nose, sketching,
in your mind, a portrait
of lips on skin.

> I imagine nights,
> fingers bent on F sharp,
> when your trumpet
> trembled and crooned
> sweet delta blues.

Today you sit alone
in your room with your
metal cross, your trumpet
retired. And your mahogany
mirror that's hung so clean
on cracked plaster walls
reflects our caustic age.

> You want to return,
> you want the old
> burn back, when
> clubs and streets
> were packed with bodies
> that would drip
> just from listening.

We Do This

Listening with indifference to the cries of those who perish because they are after all just barbarians killing each other

And the lives of the well-fed are worth more than the lives of the starving.

—Czesław Miłosz

History is never kind
to muted voices, to the *other*
kind, even when heated,
their words are sublimated
never sublime. We write them
wrongly, wrong them,
crush them, ignore them, mostly.
Who they are
we'll never know
or show them we do
when we do,
even in that brief
moment when that something
in their eye
lets us see their human
side, their tortured
mind. If we relate,
we'll see the stakes,
but it's too late,
justice is not just
blind: it's deaf too.
If we put an ear
to the ground
we can hear
mustang-ghosts
thunder across plains.
But with one ear

skyward do we
not lose one of two
sound-tools?
That's how we move
from the past,
how we present
our presence:
we plane down
unsightly bumps,
smooth out
knotty surfaces.
We do this
so we can hear
like a head
dunked in ice
water, the frozen
cries, muffled,
bubble and disappear.

Mine Own Baudelaire

As a kid I read
Global Soul Mates.
It's not a book
about the lover
you're destined to run
away with or drink
Cabernet with, the person
you share your nightmares,
bodily fluids or dreams with,
but the soul mate from another
shore who looks, thinks,
acts as you do. *Somewhere in
the world everyone has
an identical twin*: such a frightening
yet romantic thing. I always pictured
my kindred spirit
as a modern day Baudelaire,
writing in an overpriced
Parisian closet. I always wonder
what we owe our other us? Imagine being
responsible for two of you:
the balance of laundry,
checkbooks and eating well,
the challenge of maintaining
sleep enough to remain employed.
Imagine, on top of this, the constant
worry that the other you
might be home, spilling coffee
on your favorite Persian rug.
      At the Post Office today,
I looked up from the *Times*
to the entire line
glaring at me. I thought they must
be staring past me, outside, at some

horrific accident, but I turned
only to find the line behind
glancing down or away.
Zipper? It would not
have been the first time.
A casual left handed brush.
No. On my way out
I stopped to put my new
Peregrine Falcon stamps on
my weekly letters to the editor
and there he was: the big green eyes,
pouty lips, (yes, I have pouty lips,)
receding hairline and clean
shaven beard. Mine own Baudelaire,
not French, not living in Paris,
possibly not a poet at all,
but from the poster I learned
of his previous employment
as the borrower of many cars;
I learned too that his *Wanted*
award was larger than my gross
income for the entire nineteen-nineties.

Cafés are Dying

Whenever I see yellow
neon at night or signs
that say *no cell phones
please*, I think of you,
painting the same scene.
Your life on Jackson Street
captured on canvas
after canvas. The sky the only thing
you changed. In some, the sun
sat high above thin clouds.
In others, the moon hung
low near lamppost-glow.
In perfect hues you kept
your building alive.
The weather-worn brick,
painted grayish-black,
cornices, flecks of reddish-brown,
the upstairs windows,
shades of blue, in gold the neon
flash of wings, the sign
for your Busy-Bee Café.
To move you from Jackson
took your passing.
My memories of that time
now live in these repeated scenes,
the unframed paintings still stacked
in careful rows in your sister's house.
Strange now to think
how in your painted world
people never appeared,
only shadows behind
your apartment windows
and an empty café.
Your sister called today,

said *The Herald*'s cover
showed a picture of your
old place; the headline read:
City Condemns Old Landmark,
The Busy-Bee Café, Not So Busy Now.

For Your Horse

In Toronto sleep with Batman
nightlights in every dark room;
your nightgown will shine
like the evaporated
sheen on the coat of your
draft horse. Offer mud to everyone
near the jungle gym, offer sage
advice to the swings,
jump ropes, flagpoles
and lawyers. In your endless will
leave almost everything
to yourself, but leave
carrots, shotguns, and history
for your horse. Mornings alone,
eat chocolate cake
wearing nothing
but hairpins.
Picture pumpkin
tornadoes, cornless
summers, become an official
counter for the counties'
annual blade of grass
counting championship.
Leave your homework,
finished, at the bank.
Picture your tombstone
on the Isle of Capri.
Then drive through
town real slow-like,
waving to everyone,
your crooked glasses,
silver hair, shining
in midday sun.

Liddy's Prayer Card

—for James Liddy

                          rd
May your thoughts be ha~~ppy~~

as ~~sham~~rocks

              p   s
May your ~~heart~~ ^   be filled with

     p
~~s~~ong.

                        whores
May each day bring bright ~~hours~~,

              night
that stay all the ~~year~~ long.

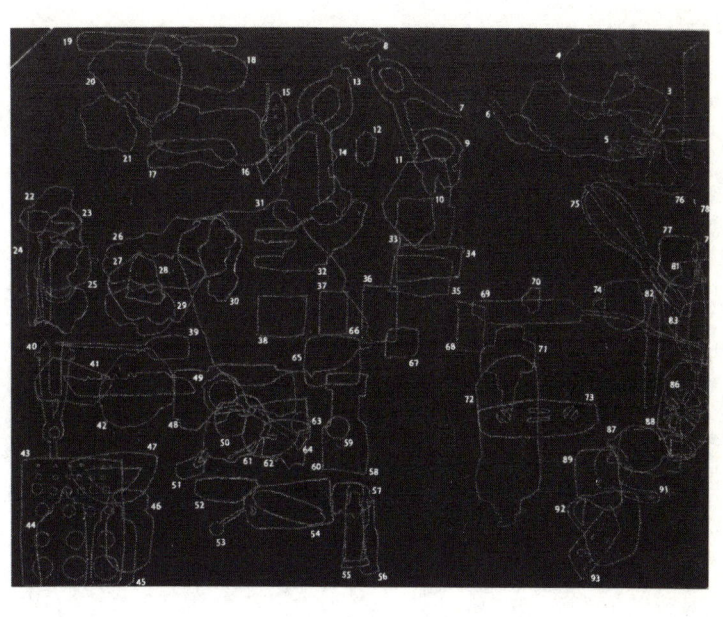

It

> *I have no words with which to tell you where I have been since I saw you last.*
>
> —Sherwood Anderson

He tells everyone he is *left
handed*, squeezing an empty
sleeve where his right arm
no longer swings. He *left* the shredded
appendage, *ditched the pieces*,
he says, *in an Afghan ditch*.
Never again will he be right
handed nor will he be right:
correct, he says, *not right*,
correcting himself: his right
now to refuse to use the word.
Different, he'd stress, this is, than to say
wounded equals *weak*, or to say
he's *damaged goods*: it leans too much
on good. God now appears in groceries
dropped and fumbled keys.
Goddamn it, he says, as apples roll and eggs,
freed from their carton, break.
It. Goddamn *it*. *It* is
everything. The Id thrown off
balance, a new battle ensues
between Super-ego and Id:
how to remove the military
from the mind, how to rid
subconscious encounters with an IED.
Remove the E and the Id
returns and wins. Remove the D, the IE
remains, i.e....*id est...that is*. Impossible,
it is, to do. In the end, he is left
alone to carry his weightless arm.

Idle

On weeknights my father disappeared
into his windowless shed with a bottle of Schlitz
and boxes from *Frank's Salvage and Junk*.
From fifteen broken watches he'd make
two whole again—with radios and cameras
it took twenty or thirty to get one—his gifts
for birthdays and Christmases. My brother and I
begged to help, but the closed shed door
repeated his no. We only saw the remains
of this strange world—forty-six radios,
thirty watches, and ten cameras shelved
above mountains of gears and wires.
"Leave it all," he said, when his legs failed
and we sold the house. Now he has
passed from even his final
tiny room; and the city he built
in his retired idle time is still spread
across the walnut hutch, but in my
study now. He willed this toy train,
his hours of building to me, left a note
taped to the caboose in his sideways scrawl:
"you can give it to your boy,
and let him blow the damn whistle."

Winter Dogs

Tonight the sky vanished
    into an ashen wall,
heads covered in wet-white and in people's
    eyes the first flakes'
undeniable magic. At the Mayakovskaya stop,
    a babushka, drowning in her
        woolen dress is hunched
    against the metro steps;
    the cavernous descent
    as impressive as the ornamental
machine gun mosaics, weapons held in perfect
    pose by socialist warriors.
        Stalin said the metro stations
were the palaces of the people.
        On these palace steps, the babushka,
            staring into colorless sky,
    repeated to the passers by,
Pomagee karmeet sabaki *(Please help me feed these dogs.)*
        She had five hounds
        tied to the handrail.
Each one skilled in the art of sadness,
    masters of the frown,
        cringe and whimper.
    Above her, a steady drip of melted snow,
steaming warmth from women
    selling bruised fruit, blini and pelmeni.
        Then from below, a chorus of voices
            splashed into the snow-flaked air.
    Four young men appeared,
arms locked at the elbow.
    Agitated from the clamor, one of the dogs
        upturned her bucket of change,
sailing it down the steps. The woman
    whacked the dog with a paper.

One of the men flung
    his beer bottle at the woman,
screamed, "Idiot!" It shattered
against the wall and two dogs
    broke free into the gray night.

Night

All night the street will surge, but the parking lots
are empty. L.A. Wash and Tan is covered now
by roll-down gates. The Wooden Nickel's
signs for Miller and Pabst flicker blue and red
beneath milky streetlight globes; I count sixteen
before they fade, a blur down North Avenue.
As I stretch for the light, I hear a woman scream.
    Son of a bitch.
In the Nickel's parking lot she pounds
on the hood of a Buick Skylark.
    Asshole motherfucker.
She hollers and thrashes against the car
until he opens the door.
    You better not come near me.
She backs away. He walks to her, leans down
until their faces almost touch. In the dark,
their silhouetted heads become
a strange and giant heart. For a moment,
I think they will embrace. Then she screams
again and spits in his face. He knocks her down,
two punches to the mouth. Before I can
call the cops, the Buick peels out onto North,
fishtails and swerves into an oncoming truck.
I reach the street as the paramedics arrive.

New York

rain drums Fifth Avenue
and maple leaves fall
heavy on windshields
begging to be let in

men selling umbrellas
appear from nowhere
like worms that slip
from burrows onto sidewalks

golden drums pound
in boroughs and down avenues
as we stand in black and hammer
back smiles in the dust
filled dusk and bones like antlers
sink with worms in the rain

Before the Bookcase

Bury me in a bookcase
coffin: Abbot's hammer,
Melleray oak. Bury me
when *the small rain* never
touches ground and great
blue herons land in lolling
Mississippi backwater.
Bury me in a scene I can't
describe like a hand
unshaken, like an idea lost
under the bed for years,
lost like rectory dust.
Sister Mary is cleaning again,
the dust and my sins.
What is the penance
for dying? Coffin-dirt-clods
sound like trumpet
swans dropping eggs.
The fox is asleep
on the head of the hunter.
Oil my eyes
Oil my eyes
Oil my troubled ears
Unhinge the coffin,
the bookcase, my dying.

Not Anointed

i

To be my eyes
unhinged as the church door
oil these wooden pet bones

Oil my troubled ears
Jacob on water on oil
knocking for Sichar

Circling groves to the rim
squeeze olives along
nostril, lightly

Unburnish the kissed
sealing the young man
the lips-time, in vain, sealed

Start this lavabo
a hand clearer than rocky
flowing egg white

Run out athlete, soaked
rubdown both of the bedded
balm with my feet

ii

Hooking my soul there,
a shirt, air shaped, T,
tack twig on the T

The Allerton Hotel, Chicago

The sun, in a tower of light,
breaks through clouds heavy with rain,
blanching the face of a bell hop
who squints and holds up a hand

as if he were saluting the sky
or waving to the woman who,
in less than a minute,
will jump from the fifteenth floor.

He is, of course, not waving,
but waiting, like the small crowd
that has amassed to see a life disappear.
Before my mother understood

why so many people had gathered
on a gray afternoon in front of a hotel,
the woman dropped into a collective scream,
then silence, then sirens. I will not tell you

the color of the dress
that gathered around her waist,
rippled and snapping like a flag,
or the sound of her bones

folding into themselves.
What I remember—I was eight—
is not the falling, but the rows
of men and women hushed by terror.

January

In April you sang
    a sullen rhapsody,
        spring's version
            of *Round Midnight*.
    In July we slept
  in florid green,
      mosquitoes bit and beans
        climbed
    our fish-line trellis.
In October, hollowed and hardened,
        tomato plants glistened
      in morning frost.
        January now and I chop
            onions and pit olives.
                My eyes burn and fingers swim
          in garlic and ginger.
      You pour Beaujolais and we
    pretend in red vertigo.
      Snow on the way
        to the airport,
          chance for delays.
              Strong gusts sweep
      white dust across the tarmac
        as you pull away.

Hunting Eagles

Summer mornings, Uncle Leon
would take me to watch
barges scrape through the locks:
men on coolers reeling in
slick flipping catfish,
the rush of brown water
turning white over the dam.

Out on the jetty we'd scan
dense florid bluffs for eagles,
not leaving until we spotted at least
three or until mosquitoes
chased us back to the vinyl
upholstery of his blue Plymouth.

I don't remember Uncle Leon
as something broken, but I imagine
he was lonelier after he shed
the layers of cognac and gin.
I don't remember his voice,
only his eyes, excited when I
found the white heads of eagles.
I remember the binoculars'
heavy steel and how the curved glass
could lift me from where I stood.

Two Mornings on Avenida 9 de Julio

Steady rain on the streets of Buenos Aires,
summer dust now wet and earthy.
Under the canopy of the Café Viridita,
pigeons, fat and lustrous as passion fruit,
peck the freshly washed sidewalk.
As I move towards them, they rise
for only a moment, and cooing, they land
around me, spread out like a blue-gray sea.
Farther on, outside the Teatro Colón,
under an umbrella, a man opens two suitcases,
puts up a sign: "Troca con Leandro"—
busts of Eva Perón on pins, leather wallets,
Italian pocket watches, and postcards of La Recoleta.
I pick out a watch—tarnished silver, the chain
long and golden. Leandro shakes his head,
no quieres eso, es viejo. Aquí, aquí, éste es mejor.
I buy the old one—the warm circle of it
in my palm feels, in a way I can't explain,
familiar—not like walking home from work
past the same neon lit store fronts,
the same brick houses, the random
purple door, no longer random, and into
the sound of your children
shrieking above the evening news;
it's something different. Or maybe it's not
familiar at all—maybe it's that I hope
its years can unfold a city that is a mystery
only to me, or that it will make me
not seem like the newest thing here;
Leandro laughs at my choice and throws
in a pin of Evita. I open the watch, wind it,
set the time, wait for the tick-tock-tick.

§

Across the charge of traffic
a young boy lies on his stomach
on the boulevard's matted grass,
his arms, a tripod, his hands like wings,
v-shaped under his chin. In front of him
on the damp green, two oranges, sticky
along thin breaks of skin, a green apple,
bruised brown. When the lights turn red
he jumps to his feet, moves from car to car
juggling the fruit high into the air.
He closes his eyes, does not miss.
Then a woman, talking on her phone,
her high heels clacking against the pavement,
knocks the child down, fruit rolling under a car,
"¡Maldita!" she yells, and hurries
across the street. Stunned, the child gets up
just before the lights turn back to green.

Will He Not Recall

> *Little as I knew you I know you: little as you knew me you know me*
>
> —Adrienne Rich

As you lift the body off the floor,
grayish-red clouds moving north,
you put a stranger's face on
your wife.
    As this stranger lies
limp in your arms,
you watch yourself tell
your son his mother
is gone. Does your soul
scream red-barbed-wire
as you wait for no
one to take her place?
    Will the soldier, his weapon
retired, picture you
like this? Will he not recall
her eyes closed, her motionless
body? Will he not imagine
another son whose
world has become
a room of glass walls,
reflecting, as he can't
turn away, his life to come?

From Grace to Goshen

On Friday nights my father, manic, cut
coupons and cleared shelf space in the barn—
rows of box-fans, light bulbs, and flashlights.
He charted his course on maps, from Grace
to Goshen, south as far as Muncie.
His old pickup truck was gone by five.
Sometimes he'd drive a thousand miles in two days,
from K-Mart to K-Mart. He slept inside the cab,
then started again. The *blue-light specials*
would save him *hundreds*. On Sunday, late,
he'd drive up slow, a haze in front of headlights,
the dust drummed up from the gravel road.
He sat in the truck, sometimes for hours,
before he'd start to unload, down by weekend's close.

Flocks of Never

We had to throw things
away to sell our house,
make it seem like we lived
sparingly—a minimalist life.
As if anyone lives
with only one blue shirt
in the closet,
one pair of shoes illuminated
by a single light bulb swinging—
40 watts and a string to pull,
frayed twine and a soundless
plastic bell, to turn it on,
to turn it off.

For years I watched ivy
spread over my neighbor's house.
Each year the leaves
turned from green to red
to gone. When the leaves
fell, flocks of never
migrating starlings
ate the purple berries,
tugged off the stems.

For years, from my kitchen window,
I watched Siberian snow geese
winter along the Columbia River.
Each day they'd rise
like heavy rain clouds blown by wind—
white plumage like morning sky,
black wings like shadows,
like rain. Sometimes, so early, the sky
still the color of ashy smoke,
thousands of geese would disappear
into a whorl of sudden snow.
In these moments, I'd imagine,
though I never saw anything

like it, the spray of twelve gauge
buckshot entering the body
of a goose in mid-air,
and its mate, its mate for life,
would honk, drop down,
honk, follow the limp body
to the ground.
And because this is
a love story,
the falling goose,
the following goose,
the strange replaying of this scene,
the replaying of something
that did not happen,
never disturbed me,
the way it does now,
as I stand in my new house,
in my new closet
with no string to pull.
Instead a switch, like all the other
modern rooms, easier I suppose,
to turn the light on, to turn it off.
And strangely, with no geese
at my new kitchen window,
I have traded scenes: the repeated falling
goose for the last moment
in my old closet. Standing in the dark,
even my blue shirt gone,
I pull the string a final time.
I turn the light on to dust
in the corner, turn it off
to the empty dark,
thinking, how the severity of nothing
can fill up a room.
And because I can not resist
I turn it on and turn it off
again and again, like I did
when I was five, maybe four,
when the simplicity of light
and dark was enough
to stay an afternoon.

Notes

Dedication: for my parents and their will to live through a horrifying night and beyond.

Epigraphs: Roberto Bolaño, "Dirty, Poorly Dressed." Trans. Laura Healy. René Char, "Mourning at Nevons." Trans. Laure Schmitz.

"Silent": Wisława Szymborska, "Miracle Fair." Trans. Joanna Trzeciak.

"Son": H.D., "Tribute to the Angels."

"New Orleans": the photograph "Blind DeDe Pierce – one of the last old New Orleans Jazz men," by Leonard Freed was published in *Black in White America* (New York, 1968).

"We Do This": Czesław Miłosz, "Sarajevo."

"Liddy's Prayer Card": this poem is taken from a prayer card that I found in a book James gave to me. The card is from St. Patrick's Church in Whitewater, Wisconsin. The edits are James' and the poem appears here as an homage to his work, life, and generosity.

"It": Sherwood Anderson, "A New Testament: X."

"Before the Bookcase" and "Not Anointed": these poems are tributes to the poet Raymond Roseliep. In "Before the Bookcase," *The Small Rain* refers to his 1963 collection of poems. "Not Anointed" is a reworking of his poem, "Anointed."

"Will He Not Recall": Adrienne Rich, "Inscriptions."

"From Grace to Goshen": is dedicated to the writer and artist, Jim Walker.

About the Author

DREW BLANCHARD holds a BA in Journalism from the University of Iowa and an MFA in poetry from The Ohio State University. He is currently a PhD candidate in English at the University of Wisconsin-Milwaukee where he has twice been awarded The Academy of American Poets Prize. In January of 2009 he received a university research grant to work with the novelist Iván Thays in Lima, Perú and in the summer of 2010 he was a graduate student scholar at the National University of Ireland, Maynooth, a scholarship provided by the International Association for the Study of Irish Literatures. His writing has appeared in *Best New Poets, Notre Dame Review, Guernica / a magazine of art & politics, Blackbird, Meridian* and elsewhere. *Winter Dogs* is his debut collection.